RUBANK EDUCATIONAL LIBRARY No. 180

T0071507

FRENCH HORN

VOL. II

WM. GOWER

AND

H. VOXMAN

**AN OUTLINED COURSE OF STUDY
DESIGNED TO FOLLOW UP ANY
OF THE VARIOUS ELEMENTARY
AND INTERMEDIATE METHODS**

HAL•LEONARD®
CORPORATION
7777 W. BLUEMOUND RD. P.O. BOX 13819 MILWAUKEE, WI 53213

NOTE

THE RUBANK ADVANCED METHOD for French Horn is published in two volumes, the course of study being divided in the following manner:

Vol. I
{ Keys of C, F, G, B♭, and D Major.
{ Keys of A, D, E, G, and B Minor.

Vol. II
{ Keys of E♭, A, A♭, E, D♭, and B Major.
{ Keys of C, F#, F, and C# Minor.

PREFACE

THIS METHOD is designed to follow any of the various Elementary and Intermediate instruction series, or Elementary instruction series comprising two or more volumes, depending upon the previous development of the student. The authors have found it necessary in their teaching experience to draw from many sources in order to provide a progressive course of study. The present publication assembles in two volumes the material essential to a well-rounded musical development.

THE OUTLINES, one of which is included in each of the respective volumes, tend to afford an objective picture of the student's progress. They will facilitate the ranking of members in a large ensemble or they may serve as a basis for awards of merit. In addition, a one-sided development along strictly technical or strictly melodic lines is avoided. The use of these outlines, however, is not imperative and they may be discarded at the discretion of the teacher.

NOTATION: Music for the French Horn is written in both the treble and bass clefs. In the bass clef two manners of notation are employed, the old and the new:

In this method the new notation is used throughout.

Wm. Gower — H. Voxman

Table of Harmonics for French Horn

The seventh harmonic is too flat and the eleventh harmonic is too sharp to be used satisfactorily.

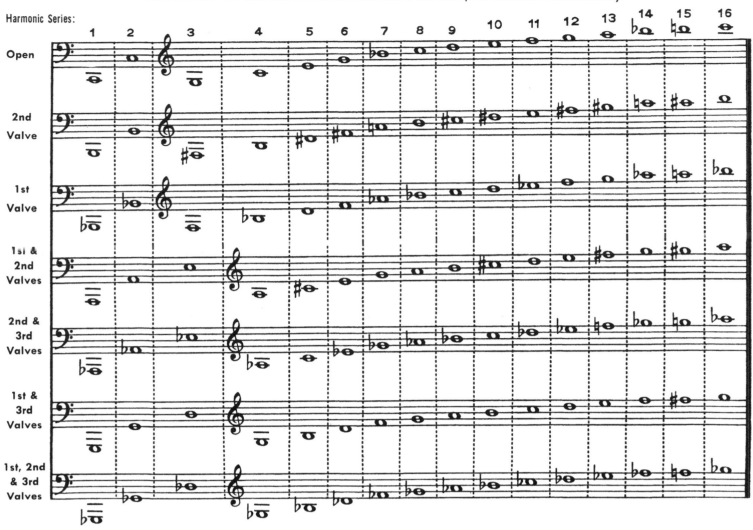

Chromatic Fingering Chart

Regular fingerings are for the F Horn; parenthetical fingerings are for the Bb Horn. The *Third Valve* may be used as an alternate fingering for the *First and Second Valves* on either the F Horn or the Bb Horn.

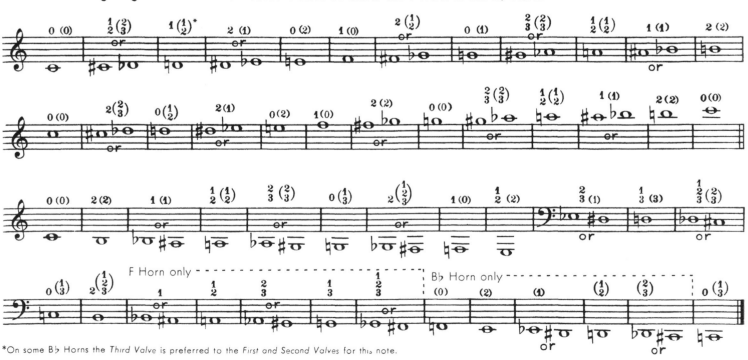

*On some Bb Horns the *Third Valve* is preferred to the *First and Second Valves* for this note.

PRACTICE AND GRADE REPORT

SECOND SEMESTER

Student's Name _____   Date _____

Week	Sun.	Mon.	Tue.	Wed.	Thu.	Fri.	Sat.	Total	Parent's Signature	Grade
1										
2										
3										
4										
5										
6										
7										
8										
9										
10										
11										
12										
13										
14										
15										
16										
17										
18										
19										
20										

Semester Grade _____

Instructor's Signature _____

FIRST SEMESTER

Student's Name _____   Date _____

Week	Sun.	Mon.	Tue.	Wed.	Thu.	Fri.	Sat.	Total	Parent's Signature	Grade
1										
2										
3										
4										
5										
6										
7										
8										
9										
10										
11										
12										
13										
14										
15										
16										
17										
18										
19										
20										

Semester Grade _____

Instructor's Signature _____

OUTLINE
OF
RUBANK ADVANCED METHOD
FOR
FRENCH HORN, Vol. II
BY
Wm. Gower and H. Voxman

UNIT	SCALES and ARPEGGIOS	(Key)	MELODIC INTERPRE-TATION	ARTICU-LATION	FLEXIBILITY and TONGUING		ORNA-MENTS	SOLOS	UNIT COM-PLETED
1	6 (1) 7 (5)	Eb	20 (1)	43 (1)	55 (1)	62 (1)	67 (1)	73 (1)	
2	6 (2) 7 (6)	Eb	21 (2)	43 (2)	55 (1)	62 (1)	67 (1)	73 (1)	
3	6 (3) 7 (7)	Eb	22 (3)	44 (3)	55 (1)	62 (2)	67 (2)	73 (1)	
4	7 (4) (8)	Eb	22 (4)	44 (4)	55 (2)	62 (3)	67 (3)	73 (1)	
5	8 (9)	c	23 (5)	44 (5)	55 (2)	62 (4)	67 (3)	73 (1)	
6	8 (10)	c	24 (6)	45 (6)	55 (3)	62 (4)	67 (4)	73 (1)	
7	8 (11) (12) (13)	c	24 (7)	45 (6)	56 (4)	62 (5)	67 (4)	74 (2a)	
8	8 (14) 10 (18)	A	25 (8)	45 (7)	56 (5)	62 (5)	68 (5)	74 (2a)	
9	9 (15) 10 (19)	A	26 (9)	45 (8)	56 (6)	63 (6)	68 (5)	74 (2a)	
10	9 (16) 10 (20)	A	26 (9)	46 (9)	56 (7)	63 (6)	68 (6)	74 (2b)	
11	9 (17) 10 (21)	A	27 (10)	46 (9)	56 (8)	63 (7)	68 (7)	74 (2b)	
12	10 (22) 11 (24)	f#	28 (11)	46 (10)	56 (9)	63 (7)	68 (7)	74 (2b)	
13	10 (23)	f#	28 (12)	46 (11)	56 (9)	63 (8)	69 (8)	75 (3)	
14	11 (25) (26) (27)	f#	28 (12)	46 (11)	56 (9)	63 (8)	69 (9)	75 (3)	
15	11 (28)	Ab	29 (13)	47 (12)	57 (10)	64 (9)	69 (9)	75 (3)	
16	12 (29) (32)	Ab	29 (13)	47 (13)	57 (10)	64 (9)	69 (10)	75 (3)	
17	12 (30) 13 (33)	Ab	30 (14)	48 (14)	57 (10)	64 (9)	69 (11)	75 (3)	
18	12 (31) 13 (34)	Ab	30 (15)	48 (14)	57 (11) (12)	64 (10)	69 (11)	75 (3)	
19	13 (35) (38)	f	31 (16)	48 (15)	57 (11) (12)	64 (10)	70 (12)	76 (4)	
20	13 (36) 14 (39)	f	32 (17)	49 (16)	57 (13) (14)	64 (11)	70 (13)	76 (4)	
21	13 (37) 14 (40) (41)	f	32 (17)	49 (17)	57 (13) (14)	64 (11)	70 (13)	76 (4)	
22	14 (42) 15 (46)	E	32 (18)	49 (18)	58 (15)	65 (12)	70 (14)	76 (4)	
23	14 (43) 15 (47)	E	33 (19)	49 (18)	58 (16)	65 (12)	70 (15)	76 (4)	
24	15 (44) 16 (48)	E	34 (20)	50 (19)	58 (17)	65 (13)	70 (15)	76 (4)	
25	15 (45) 16 (49)	E	34 (21)	50 (20)	58 (18)	65 (14)	71 (16)	77 (5)	
26	16 (50)	c#	35 (22)	50 (21)	58 (18)	65 (14)	71 (16)	77 (5)	
27	16 (51)	c#	35 (22)	51 (22)	59 (19)	65 (15)	71 (17)	77 (5)	
28	16 (52) (53) (54)	c#	36 (23)	51 (23)	59 (19)	65 (15)	71 (17)	77 (5)	
29	16 (55) 17 (60)	Db	37 (24)	52 (24)	60 (20)	66 (16)	71 (18)	77 (5)	
30	17 (56) (57) 18 (61)	Db	38 (25)	52 (25)	60 (20)	66 (16)	71 (18)	77 (5)	
31	17 (58) 18 (62)	Db	39 (26)	52 (25)	60 (21)	66 (17)	72 (19)	79 (6)	
32	17 (59) 18 (63)	Db	39 (26)	53 (26)	60 (21)	66 (17)	72 (19)	79 (6)	
33	18 (64)	B	40 (27)	53 (27)	61 (22)	66 (18)	72 (20)	79 (6)	
34	18 (65) 19 (67)	B	41 (28)	54 (28)	61 (22)	66 (18)	72 (20)	79 (6)	
35	19 (66) (68)	B	42 (29)	54 (29)	61 (23)	66 (19)	72 (20)	79 (6)	
36	19 (69) (70)	B	42 (29)	54 (30)	61 (23)	66 (19)	72 (20)	79 (6)	

NUMERALS designate page number.

ENCIRCLED NUMERALS designate exercise number.

COMPLETED EXERCISES may be indicated by crossing out the rings, thus, ⊗.

1456-75

Scales and Arpeggios

Eb Major

1456-75

Various articulations may be used in the chromatic, the interval, and the arpeggio exercises.

Chromatic Scale

Scale in Thirds

Common Chord

Dominant 7th Chord

C Minor

Practice with different articulations.

29

simile

simile

30

31

Scale in Thirds

32

14

Scale in Thirds

39

Common Chord

40

Diminished 7th Chord

41

E Major

42

simile

simile

43

Chromatic Scale

Scale in Thirds

16

1456-75

Chromatic Scale

18

Scale in Thirds
Practice also an octave lower

61

Common Chord
Practice both octaves

62

Dominant 7th Chord

63

B Major

64

simile

simile

65

simile

simile

Studies in Melodic Interpretation
For One or Two Part Playing

The following studies have been selected with the idea of ensemble performance in mind. Much effort has been expended in selecting duets in which the first and second parts are melodically and rhythmically independent. Students should be encouraged to practice these numbers as duets outside of the lesson period. When circumstances permit, any number of students can perform them as an ensemble. The lower part of the duets may be assigned at the discretion of the teacher.

Careful attention to the marks of expression is essential to effective use of the material. Where different dynamic signs are written for the upper and lower parts, observe them accurately. The part having the melody must always slightly predominate even when the dynamic indications are the same.

Pencil the technically difficult passages and devote extra time to their mastery.

In rhythmic music in the more rapid tempi (marches, dances, etc.), tones that are equal divisions of the beat are played somewhat detached (staccato). Tones that equal a beat or are multiples of a beat are held full value. Tones followed by rests are usually held full value. This point should be especially observed in slow music.

Gigue

CHEDEVILLE

FRANZ

1456-75

HANDEL

SCHUBERT

BRANEUX

Allegretto

5

SICILIENNE

GALLAY

GOSTINELLI

Larghetto (♩= 96)

MOZART

mp legato

8

a little slower

MELODY

SAMBATARO

GOSTINELLI

BRANEUX

ECHO MINUET and AIR

18th Century

PIETZSCH

GEMINIANI

Poco agitato

ROSSARI

17

A. BELLOLI

Adagio

18

JIGG

SNOW

19

Allegro

HAYDN

20

Allegro vivace

PIETZSCH

21

MARIANO

22

Presto

18th Century

23

HUNTING SONG

SAMBATARO

24

PASTORALE

KRANZ

PIETZSCH

Allegro non tanto

26

A TRUMPET MARCH

18th Century

27

RAMAIN

28

29

Andante espressivo (in six)

Studies in Articulation

The material for this section has been taken for the most part from various standard publications for brass instruments.

Play the exercises as quickly as technic permits unless otherwise indicated.

44

49

MENDELSSOHN
(adapted)

Flexibility Exercises

Students having a double horn should practice on F horn only.

1456-75

56

Play Exercises 9 & 10 in strict time at increasing speeds and also as accelerated trills.

1456-75

Work for an even attack and a steady dynamic level.

22

Andante placido   VECCHIETTI

23

Tonguing Exercises

TRIPLE TONGUING and DOUBLE TONGUING

Triple tonguing is used when triplets are to be played at a speed that is too fast for single tonguing. The pattern of syllables used for this kind of tonguing is: Tu Tu Ku, Tu Tu Ku, etc.

Double tonguing is used when duplets are to be played at a speed that is too fast for single tonguing. The pattern of syllables in this case is: Tu Ku, Tu Ku, etc.

To develop a technique for either Triple or Double Tonguing it is **recommended** that the Ku attacks be practiced separately **from** the Tu attacks until a good tone can be produced on both syllables. The student may then proceed to combine the Tu and Ku, being particularly careful that both syllables sound equally distinct. It is advisable to practice slowly at first in order to produce an evenly articulated rhythm. Increase to a faster tempo only as perfection is reached.

PREPARATORY STUDIES

TRIPLE TONGUING

DOUBLE TONGUING

Musical Ornamentation (Embellishments)

ARBAN

PARÈS

68

Be sure to play the mordent squarely on the beat:

1456-75

Long Grace Notes (Appoggiatura)

* The <u>general rule</u> is that appoggiatura attached to a note value divisible by three receive two-thirds of the value of the principal note, even though their arithmetical value may be less.

The Turn (Gruppetto)

ARBAN

In the music of the time of Bach and Handel (1685-1759), cadences frequently contain the rhythmic figure ⬚ or ⬚. The time value of the dot is not trilled, the execution being ⬚ etc. It should be added that the trills of this period should generally begin with the upper note of the trill.

SOLOS
Farewell Serenade*

W. HERFURTH, Op. 85

1

Andante

*Piano accompaniment to this Solo is included in the Piano book to the "Concert and Contest Collection for Horn."

1456-75

Two Songs
I. Liebestreu
(Faith of Love)

J. BRAHMS, Op. 3, No.1

II. Tambourliedchen
(Song of the Drummer Boy)

J. BRAHMS, Op. 69, No. 5

Chanson des Chasseurs

(Song of the Hunters)

SCHUBERT - GALLAY

Wiegenlied
(Berceuse)

RICHARD STRAUSS, Op. 41, No.1

1456-75

Third Movement
from Concerto No. 2 in Eb

W. A. MOZART, K. 417

1456-75

Konzertstück

PAUL HOLZNER, Op. 23